TWIST

PIPPA LITTLE
T W I S T

2017

Published by Arc Publications
Nanholme Mill, Shaw Wood Road,
Todmorden OL14 6DA, UK
www.arcpublications.co.uk

Copyright © Pippa Little, 2017
Copyright in the present edition © Arc Publications, 2017
Design by Tony Ward
Printed by TJ International, Padstow, Cornwall

978 1910345 88 7 (pbk)
978 1910345 89 4 (hbk)
978 1910345 90 0 (ebk)

Cover image:
'Imparium', 2014, by Caitlin T. McCormack,
by kind permission of the artist.

This book is in copyright. Subject to statutory exception
and to provision of relevant collective licensing agreements,
no reproduction of any part of this book may take place without
the written permission of Arc Publications.

Editor for the UK and Ireland:
John W. Clarke

ACKNOWLEDGEMENTS

Acknowledgements are due to the editors of the following print and online publications where some of these poems first appeared: Ambit, And Other Poems, Antiphon, Artemis, Black Light Engine Room, Butcher's Dog, Filmpoems, Glasgow Herald, Glasgow Review of Books, Gutter, Human Journal, Interlitq, London Grip, Magma, Morning Star, MsLexia, New Salzburg Review, New Writing Scotland 31, Poetica, Poetry Review, Skylark Review, The Compass, The Interpreter's House, The Lampeter Review, The North, The Ofi, The Poetry Shed, The Scotsman, The Stare's Nest, The Stockholm Review, Under The Radar and Undertow Review.

'Dark Starling' was one of the poems chosen to commemorate and explore the Scots role in slavery in Glasgow 2014. It appears in the anthology Yonder Awa. 'Moleskins' won Second Prize in the 2013 Ledbury Poetry Competition. 'How Helen Steven...' won Second Prize in the Second Light Network Poetry Competition 2014. 'Clooty Gospel' was part of Antiphonal, a project to celebrate the return of the Lindisfarne Gospels to Durham in 2013 by twelve poets. It appears in the anthology Shadowscript. 'I Think Of You And Think Of Skin' was placed in The Bridport Poetry Competition in 2013. 'Green Ginger' was commended in the Larkin and East Riding Competition, 2014. 'Auld Lags' was Highly Commended in the Wigtown Competition 2014. 'Smeuse' was Highly Commended in The Rialto Nature Poetry Competition 2014. 'Cobbles' was Runner-up in the Black Country Museum Poetry Competition 2013. 'Mystical Kitchens' appears in Driving Down The Lane, edited by Agnes Marton and Harriette Lawler. 'Altweibersommer' won First Prize in the Newcastle Winter Book Festival Competition in 2012. 'Scrap Metals Across Europa' won Second Prize, Wigtown, 2015. 'Back to Baltic Street' was in The Sea (Rebel Poetry Ireland), and 'I Think of You...' appeared in Hallelujah for 50ft Women (Bloodaxe), both 2015. 'Hen Party' and 'Sad Jaguar' appeared in *Our Lady of Iguanas* (Black Light Engine Room Press, 2016). 'In The Fourth Month' was published in *Writing Motherhood*, ed. Carolyn Jess-Cooke (Seren, 2017), as 'For My Miscarriage'.

    The author would like to thank The Society of Authors, The Hawthornden Foundation, New Writing North, The Newcastle University Women's Workshop, Carte Blanche and Bob Little.

for Jane, my sister

CONTENTS

Altweibersommer / 13
Elisabeth Says / 14
The Fortunate Isles / 15
I And The Village / 16
Snail Shells / 17
Black Middens / 18
Stilt-Walking The Tyne / 19
Riddle With Two Answers / 20
Auld Lags / 22
Cobbles / 23
Chainsaw Music / 24
Our Lady's Threads / 25
Turn and Turn / 26
I Think of You and Think of Skin / 27
Mystical Kitchens / 28
For Adele / 29
Moleskins / 30
One With Another / 31
The Cartographer's Morning-After Shirt / 32
Grace Poole Fits A Toile / 33
Green Ginger / 34
Trapdoor / 35
Stone Balancing / 36
Scrap Metals Across Europa / 37
How Helen Steven… / 38
Moss Side Public Laundry 1979 / 39
In Hope / 40
Brushing the Old Yellow Lab / 41
Mami Wata / 42
Flower of Maryam / 44
Net / 46
One for Sorrow / 47
Clast / 48

Dark Starling / 50
Southernness Point / 51
Stump and Phantom / 52
Smeuse / 53
Nobody's Daughter / 54
Lupin Tea / 55
Sister / 56
In The Fourth Month / 57
Zoetrope / 58
Handspeak / 59
Blotto / 60
Night Drive / 62
Hair Shirt / 63
Hen Party, Mexico City / 64
Sad Jaguar / 65
What Remained of the Wedding Cake / 66
Back to Baltic Street / 67
Clooty Gospel / 68
Suitcase Baby / 69
Scissors Give Birth to Scissors / 70
Departure / 71
Lambing / 72
Against Hate / 73
Whirlwind / 74

Notes / 76
Biographical Note / 79

Twist, from Old English (candeltwist, a "wick"); twis – from root of "two". Original senses suggest "dividing in two" (Old Norse "tvistra", to divide / separate). Later senses are of "combining two into one", hence the original sense of the word may be "thread formed by twisting, spinning or plaiting". Meaning "act or action of turning on an axis" is attested from 1576. Also "the course of a life figured as a thread".

Oxford English Dictionary

"You can't drive straight on a twisty lane"

Russian Proverb

ALTWEIBERSOMMER
Old Wives' Summer

In Altweibersommer
we gather the first misty skeins
dip them in piss-starch, dwindle and spin them into wires
that twitch with all the conversations of the world.
We may choose to drown them in a milky ditch
or whisper them home:
we have no appetite for love but dawdle where young men
rise out of clear pools, shaking drops free in golden,
needle-fine constellations – we sew them old, heart-stuffed bodies,
and when we drape the bright mesh over, each hero shivers.

In Altweibersommer
we grow weary of figs and pomegranates,
sip one another from long spoons, sigh for that honeycomb
to glisten slickly on the tongue, gulp/
gulp till the *forschung* puppy-fat is gone:
we hang shoes from elms,
snip babies' hair and set one curl in forfeit on the pillow,
knit their moth-breath into storms, throw ourselves down hills
in snarls of birds-nest, crying
prayers for cannon-food, tumbleweed, the eye-bones of
    sluttish husbands.

From the hairs on our chin we weave soft, slow, snowdrifts
that numb the flail and weathervane
in spiderly baptismal shawls or shrouds
through which dirty light frays, in, out,
in, out, like lungs, breathing.

ELISABETH SAYS
for Elisabeth Olin

Elisabeth says
as we sit together
over bowls rosy pink
that in Sweden, when children
swallow a key or some such thing,
this rhubarb is their cure: the hairy fibres
seize the object, wrap it round,
entwine it with muscles
like boa constrictors', so thus swathed
and swaddled there's no sharp end
or impediment to the journey,
and all's well!

Elisabeth says
in her experience it works
for dogs as much as babies, and
we laugh, our table messy
with a good meal finished.
She is beautiful, how she grows old.
I remember yesterday
she showed me bark
on autumnal birch,
told me her grandmothers grated it to flour
for starvation bread,
and how it tasted.

THE FORTUNATE ISLES

A calm day but dress warmly,
there's always a nip in the air
no matter what the forecasts say.

Our boat's blue as a mussel and sweetly polished.
Don't weigh yourself down
with obstinate baggage,
the farther out
the less you'll want.

Here's a feast of everything you loved,
plenty for everyone. And
lavender everywhere to give to the water.

I'll show you moonwort and adder's tongue,
the mountains from their seaward side,
Africa through the mist.
Me, in my middle age.

I AND THE VILLAGE
   after Chagall

I love you as a circle loves a shooting star
And you are mine as a bride is

Croon of my heart, you sing me stepping-stones
And you are mine as a blind eye is

I love you as a spice box craves the Sabbath
And you are mine as your instep is

Over the moon and far away home
Each word is the same word is

I love you as milk loves to be lapped
And you are mine as the bucket is

I love you as rose light is necessary to skin
And you are mine as its lullaby is.

Over the sun and into the dark
Each word is the same word and at the same time another is.

SNAIL SHELLS

The orchard wall wears them like lumpy knitting,
greys and browns, shades of afternoon
and autumn clouds. Soon they will slip away
into tea-coloured undergrowth, stony
thumb-prints, slow almost to standstill,
their tarnished silver spooling through yarrow's
last foils and curls of summer, scent on the air
of snow. So they go
and are gone one morning, the rosy bricks bare.
It will take time to find them, rolled up
in a compost nest, small beads from a lost hoard.
Sealed and dreaming, they hardly breathe, each
heartbeat slow as faraway thunder. They are whole now,
curl inside, head first, into their own dusk.

First fresh days of southern winds and snowdrops,
trails appear on tree bark, faded tinsel
in remembrance of snow-melt
that may bring you upon remains,
echoey as staircases in abandoned houses,
interiors still warm. They lie in black
overwintered grass, rocking like small boats
at your touch, springing back
as if eager for a new tide.
You can almost make out messages
scrawled in some lost script
inside, smaller and smaller spirals.

BLACK MIDDENS

Crows flap the cold towards us
coming in low on undertakers' coat-tails.
Snow smells of tin soured by mountain water
and blood's black glaze on a dropped-too-soon's
sodden tangle that never got warm,
picked blue in the ditch to innocent bone
by February's end, forgotten.

Years since we came to church.
Sins and secrets, long-winded as the river
on its stony course, do their disappear, dissolve
in us. Attend their own purpose.

STILT-WALKING THE TYNE
after an engraving by Thomas Bewick

Other laden-down days
I walk downstream to Cherryburn Bridge
but a day like today, with May's kiss on it,
I steal my father's stilts. (He's away hunting

over the valley side for poor, hot-blooded creatures).
First I cram up my skirts,
hopeful nobody's watching
and once on, a first slip and slant,

I ride the river as if she were a mare
I know could startle and unseat me,
though I sense where she's uneasiest and try
to cause her no distress, print my weight

lightly, leave no mark more
than a spill of air along the surface,
take my chances as a crane-fly might
on loose-jointed tiptoe

for I'm giantess now, can see far,
hedge over hedge to farm roofs and spire.
She's brown as a cloud and fast,
rears up with me, wily, only I can test

each step before I take it,
my head in sky, neither bird nor fish but
(before I'm all-forgetting, dry shoes,
dry land and all behind me)

I'll summon this day forward, the rest of my life,
how set loose by one another
winged and bridled
we gave ourselves the distance.

RIDDLE WITH TWO ANSWERS

What is it but

a hall or hame: in winters hackle-laden
with thorny haberdashery,
in high summer, cobweb cupboards'
handsels of love-entangle, heliotropes –

who helms this hotch-potch,
this crinkle-crankle habitation?
Who sews the hem
haphazard, who braids with tendril, hyphen,
who hitches it together, broached and bridled,

homespun handenhold,
the heart's deep holt?
What loops and leads one within another home,
more than its sum, sore through long dissolve of frost,
dreich as an abandoned nest, pin-prick of sorrows:

is nothing but a labour, a common commonplace:
bent, bowed, knocked, cut back, but
still fusing into new, season after season,
maze where small birds sing,
a tower of Babel, a secret helter-skelter,

a breathing loom
through which dark, myriad shuttles dart,
silver strands that for one moment and for perpetuity
pin the evening star inside its cage:
what but this

brilliant, difficult,
open-ended conversation of itself,
how it grew from its own growing,
sorrow-hardy but hopeful yet –
in all its brangling, over-brimming?

AULD LAGS
    Barlinnie Prisoners visit Kerrera Island
    Parrot Sanctuary, Argyll

Each dusk the ferry goes farther,
last light an arc, unsteady, strobing the wash.
Visitors leave us their voices
to settle and fade. Some smoulder on,
give us bad dreams
for most of us cannot be hushed or comforted now:
when we kiss we draw blood,
the lingo never charms for long
and our own language has too much jungle in it –
but when the Bar-L boys bring us their gutturals and jackets
hand-tacked in sail cloth for suicide watch,
nurse us gingerly like thorned bouquets
between knuckles of LOVE and HATE,
we are none of us able to summon back the ferry,
unpick the paths that brought us here,
unsay what cried out.

COBBLES

I love walking them late rainy nights,
their slippery fish-scale sheen lit from within,
love to listen to their mutter under my boot-soles,
how they unbalance me
yet hold –

they came from reefs
languorous and murky, settling slow
in a warm mineral broth
studded with trilobites, flurried
by silver tail-to-fin-to-tail
oozing into stone

and now
like shoulders in a crowd or
a house of cards, delicate
weight with counterweight,
each one alone yet borne along in shoals,
they roll me home.

CHAINSAW MUSIC

And when you were small
we stepped on shadows-only
for three blocks,
our crazy hopscotch
in dusty afternoons
that smudged our hems,
made us smell of road –
I was big enough to reach you
plums snarled in a shark-tooth fence
to jam their maroon glut later
between each other's lips –

we listened for chainsaw music
behind Lister's wood yard,
ran away unscreaming
from his watchdog's yawn.
Your shoes shone
and your mother loved you:

perhaps God won't mind
if I pretend to be a church
when you lie down
in the imaginarium of here,
the two of us so tired
and over the railway, always,
the unavoidable house,
all its windows open.

OUR LADY'S THREADS

I live low, go far and quicken
   have no mother or father
but the marsh and ditches

my lovers are Jack-Jump-About,
   Beggary, Archangel.
I weave bittercress with day's eye,

brew burdock for dog-dreams
   go leery under curfew
to where I ought not linger:

cut me down with your righteous sear
   still I return many-fold
to your skin, I stink you out.

I have no pretty songs
   like crows and heron
to whittle into music,

only my sisters, those you summon,
   quickgrass, wickens, twist –
constant as bondagers.

TURN AND TURN
Moon Watches Earth

She's a whirl,
a well-head's
surge of white,
which way
curls her feather-tail of storms?
Which tight twist
pulls clockwise
or widdershins,
Coriolis to her equator?
How the crystals shiver
in her wedding hat
as she circle dances!
How small and silver-dented
are her sad tarantellas!

I am umbilical and dark.
Energies in me, deep-burned,
thrash unseen, grind themselves in.
I remember everything.
Turn and turn and turn,
snake-tail mouth in a Mobius impasse.
I want wild tides sometimes
to make me simple,
muscle-cut. Yet my nature
loves its wonky spirals
almost surfacing beneath the skin.

I THINK OF YOU AND THINK OF SKIN

I think of you and think of skin –
its soft stretch, ways it may fold, or be pressed,
occasionally tear. How it absorbs the fix it's in,
ends up not innocent, unkissed, yet simple in its rest –
your father's work, to expose such by the sun,
harried and tawed and dressed for the intent
of its disguise with musks and roses. For you, years gone,
I'm pale now, peeled, unwritten-on, a reproach unmeant –
white widow in my quilled intransigence, a swan
alone. Days such as these, late summer of my life,
I wonder at this want to turn a yearling's tongue
to subtleties so hollow, telling tender lies –
those nights you travelled me with words, blood-nibbed
and burning, tell me I was your first, flawed, outlawed script.

MYSTICAL KITCHENS
for Leonora Carrington

Leonora's is red. A crow sits on her shoulder
while she mixes and cuts. Smoke hoods her,
cinnamon and linseed her invocations.
Her table is round as the alchemical rose,
softly layered in furry lips: she can push her arms in
to the elbow, breathe and disappear.

Miriam's is *nigredo*. Lightning's neon eels
hiss from sealed alembics, moths strike sparks
against the steel walls of her veil. She grinds dark noises
into glue, grinds and grinds
till leaden blue ignites, scuffling, squeaking,
to drops of silver honey –

Storms gather in the corners of my kitchen:
clusters of skull garlic cannot calm them.
The oven is black as a cave, deep as a mineshaft.
Under my skirts the two-headed child dreams rookeries,
gantries, licks char from the fingers of his giantess
like a cat. He and I are mute, listen for

my sisters come at first light to the circle
with mists and whispers extricated
from the aludel that's cool now,
salt-trails from a tide far out,
pale flowers of human breath
for his heart's furnace.

FOR ADELE
Remembering Carlotta

When Sister was ill
with the weakening and the thinning
and the wakening to drifts on her pillow
you buzz-cut in solidarity,
sent photos,
got your plane ticket –
yet despite the jokes
roots of the skull show through,
for people unprepared
you didn't always want to explain.

Then instead of reunion
this long trip to her funeral.
You refuse to hide your head in church:
winter ekes itself out,
your hair grows soft, new
as snowdrops.

MOLESKINS

In the company of a dog and my own dark
I took the hill road from Rothbury
through snell wind, steady rain

and regarding what I saw
at the curve of the road
on and on along the wire

– those small cocoons
two-thumbed lonely things
velvet of underearth –

brought to mind
some orrery,
an inward-looking universe:

I imagined, for no reason,
Radnoti's greatcoat
in his shallow grave,

sodden to a soft black so
deep and starless
it might seem like nothing, like falling,

to slip your hand inside:
all things struggle
like particles, lead filings, not to fly apart.

ONE WITH ANOTHER

To each the weathervane and the mast.
    A horse and his brother.
    As many fingers as the hand.
    The wild sky and the tin can.
To each the settled score or else the last laugh.

To each love's fine feather in a new hat.
    Strong rope enough for hanging.
    All the graves and graces.
    The world and its sweet marrow.

To each one life alone, long as it lasts.
    Sherbert consolations.
    Morningstar and the singing of.
    Seed in the seedbed.
To each and all of us the glory and the trespass.

THE CARTOGRAPHER'S MORNING-AFTER SHIRT

Early, before you rise, I slip away
and in the pearly morning
hold this show-through up against the light,

journey through latitudes
of meadows and upland farms,
pleated railways that fan out
to cities, aerial mosaic of darts and notches
end-on-end: I scent espresso, coinage
and tarmac until tears sting,

stumble where the grain line swoops
to hummock of each breast
and its neat trig summit,
trace meander of buttons and sewn lips,
parted, that ache for their kiss:

now longitudes of greens, golds,
loose and limber, the almost indivisible waves
that lift and fall,
huge Idaho wheatfield
tensile in a summer breeze –

here somewhere, hiding,
you have erased the scale
and I may never get home.

GRACE POOLE FITS A TOILE

I swear the stones ooze salt on nights like these,
they would drag themselves back to their deep beds
if they could. I know the rising wind

makes her fingers itch to sink half moons in my flesh.
For last resort I drag out my coffin box,
unloose that fire-licked thing from its tissue caul

and obedient, she lifts each arm to skin the rabbit of her
 seamy linen,
bare and brown, marine, she's no goddess rising from
 her shell –
Bertha, I say, word like whisky in my mouth.

Spiders' shawl drapes her, I nip and baste it,
my stitches pepper blood-drops where her nipples press
through clouded shallows, dark as the eels' nest between
 her thighs.

We stamp-dance close, my mane twists in hers, pins
stick both of us, she spins on dirty, horn-skinned feet,
tarantella, tarantella!

I pity the other one down below in her lit world, womanless,
sewing her wedding veil with a blunted needle.
But we take what we can get before high tide rolls us under.

GREEN GINGER

Low it grows in scrubs, ditches,
sucking up puddled rain, old laundry water
into varicosed roots, settles quietly
and does not advertise: does not want to be found
on account of the fog, the uproar:

brewed to a milky pus and swallowed
by sad dancers, lovers' lackeys, a dog or screw-eyed
dosser under a full moon's florid bulb, it will erase
who you are, friend, like acid splashed on flesh:
nose, eyes, neck all gone: but the sear
is within, down the windpipe, through
sacs and polyps of your trembling soul:

I've seen women wake and sing like wolves,
teeth yellow-flecked with lather, and men so
they know neither name nor home,
wandering their Land of Green Ginger, bare
and raw as the hour they were born, and as forgetting.
My father's seen sometimes in the rail yard,
strewing yellow stems along its tracks.

TRAPDOOR

I dreamed I was a room
above a trapdoor.
The room was very warm and dim.
Hanging on a rope I saw my sister
curling and circling slow in space.

She was so fair I was sorry
no-one could see how her long hair dazzled,
how her narrow legs
danced, quite bare.
Just the two of us
in that darkness.

She was about to speak
with the last of her breath
when with a terrible sound
and a rushing of air
the trapdoor fell open and down she flew.

"I'm born! I'm born!" she cried,
turning blue.
Then all was quiet and dead
in my warm room.

STONE BALANCING

Listen with your finger-ends
while the rain runs
erases
so you begin again
and something happens
surface
over
surface
cold as the farthest star
and broken war-
time radio frequencies
but a voice
you forgot you knew,
the voice of your father,
speaks through stone
grazed quartz
skin
and bone granite, a being
horned,
lamed,
lapping you with psalms.

SCRAP METALS ACROSS EUROPA

I have driven over the Pyrenees
to bring back the hearts of washing-machines,
hub-armour prised from SEATs and TOLEDOs,
the spiny innards of air con., voodoo turnings

and shavings. I know nothing of weld or seal,
having learned only how to take apart:
there is tenderness as well as lust in it:
no woman loved her cabouchons as I cherish

my used-up, lost, unwhole, lived-out charges.
I am pilgrim along cliff-edge roadways
from Compostela to a border meaningless to me,
my people are older than dusts, I wear their barbed wire rose

in my lapel. I am scented with tarnish,
meaty with aromas from the grinding wheel, I piss dark red
and cough up lightning. I'll give you a ride
as if you were my sister, my little whore sister,

dump you on the roadside for one wrong word.
I stayed for some days in Mimizan, watching
for Biscay storms, while she sat on street corners
stretching her sad accordion. Do you know how metals kiss?

By magnet. I have sung in churches
and not been washed clean. But everything finally
melts, burns, confesses. I am shepherd of my flock.
My father flayed me for my ferrous skeleton.

You ask me for my home: it has no address
but Europa, Europa. It has removable walls.
Home is where things go that will not stay.
I have picked Franco's shrapnel out of alleyways in Teruel.

I am the magpie nobody disturbs.

HOW HELEN STEVEN, PEACE ACTIVIST, SCRATCHED AN ADRIENNE RICH POEM ON HER CELL DOOR IN DUMBARTON POLICE STATION

A cell's got nothing but time in it
and a night that never grows dark.

You sit on the slab and stare at the door,
slammed from outside by a warder

who wouldn't meet your eye.
The door's scratched Pictish snarls,

first names, gang names, sex-oaths and enemies
force you to focus. But by 2 am

you can't rewrite these broke-back alphabets,
need to leave more for the next woman and the next –

words itch your palms, you
look about for some instrument –

keys taken, but you've got your jeans
so you step out of them for the zip's

metal tag and make a start;
hours it takes, most of the night, fingers

sting from the carving, but near to morning it's
complete, as much embedded in the wood

as the poet's concentrated gaze
all the while, white-hot upon your back.

MOSS SIDE PUBLIC LAUNDRY 1979

Childless, I come with a rucksack
no Silver Cross to steer topple-high
as those bare-legged women in check coats,
bulging shoes, who load and unload
hawsers of wet sheets, wring them out
to rams' horns while heat-slap of steam
dries to tinsel in our hair, frizzes our lips
gritty with Daz's sherbert dab, and the mangle
wide as a room-size remnant
never stops groaning: *one slip and you're done for…*

in the boom and echo of it all their calls swoop up
Cross-your-Hearts, Man. City socks,
crimplene pinks and rayon underskirts as
Maggie Maggie Maggie Out Out Out! blasts
from across the park, whole streets
get knocked out like teeth,
in a back alley, early, a man
jumped me, shocked as I was
by the words I could yell
which I try out now to make them laugh, these women
who scrub blood and beer and come
with red brick soap, quick-starch a party dress
while dryers flop and roar,
before their kids fly out from school
flock outside for a smoke's sweet rest
from the future bearing down,
four walls and one man.

IN HOPE
    for CMJ

I can't remember the first time I came to your house
deep-set among trees, lake stones on the step
and prayer flags prancing their wind-horse dances,

only that I came so many years
the winds frayed them and faded them,
your soul washing line

of earth yellow, blue distances,
white air, fire-red and green for the waters;
far from Nepal they withstood Northumbrian winters,

were my first sign for you, your welcome's
firecracker guffaw, our hugs, the good
rhythm of our friendship –

I touched them one by one in the rain
the day of your wake
in hope you would be free.

Three years on, the flags I hung
over the flagstones of my yard for you
grow beautiful old.

BRUSHING THE OLD YELLOW LAB

She is grainy cornfields I remember up beyond the house,
glowing on the hillsides I never reached
through late summer sunsets: long shadows in slow burn,
that longing to be somewhere else
where my life could begin. So much faster
than I expected, here I am, mothering a dog in middle-age
who slips out of herself, supple as thistledown
every season, almost-white chaff lifting in tufts,
for whom love is this wordless touch, the weight
of my hands. I plough shadows in and smooth them out,
remembering light pollen-sticky on my skin,
waiting for that sensed world to come.
Not how I thought it would be,
or enough, yet warm, rough, loose,
more than I needed.

MAMI WATA

Out of a tree's overhang
on the steamy riverside
she surprises me, offers
her crossing, then
throws her arms open
so I am stumbling down into them,
her craft startles like a colt
but she steadies me
with the hard mounds of her palms,
the smoky aromatics of her body.

Behind me he retreats, not-quite-grown son,
and instead of waiting
she throws the rope's loop into the prow,
kicks out hard into the current –
I turn and her river slurs
in lisps and whispers the gap
opening between us, milky green,
glaucous: she heaves oars against the undertow,
feet in plastic mules, thighs in loose
faded chintz, gold
at either lobe and in a molar,
fiery chink under her forehead's ravine
as she levels her gaze over my left shoulder
like a rifle.

He is slipping out from his shape,
someone else's child,
pale fold on the mosquito path
and I do nothing.

I want her to hold me,
tell me how to live
but when she makes the other landing
deft and quick, hands me out,
she curls my coins back hard
into my fist, says in my own words
Daughter, this is how it is.

FLOWER OF MARYAM
Anastatica hierochuntica

Before sunrise her first pains come:
I sit with her in stillness as
with the dying, beyond hours, days.

The body begins to open,
a clearing in a deep forest.
Now it is right I should slip this

dried-up knotted thing, sere as my
sand-blown hands and skin, into the
warm water of my bowl and watch

it uncurl, unlace again at
the familiar swell and twitch
as the cervix softens, widens.

She whispers that rainy season
returns, the sere twigs turn grey-green,
I offer her to drink, she sips

that dried-out undertaste, sweat glides
bright across her, she is ready.
It's hard for an old woman to

keep herself alive: some days are
so twisted-small and brittle. Yet
even with the dying, something

greens in me, delicately strong,
ephemerals in a desert.
Is it the gnarled cage itself that

makes new minuscule white flowers
or is it secret-seeded fruit
deep inside that breaks its bars?

The dead lie close-curled up with life.
First gleam over rooftop wires
the sun crowns, ready to push now.

NET

I am making my net
nimbly, alone:
they think I am dreaming
when my fingers twitch
like the old dog who runs again in sleep
mile upon mile, nowhere –
but I am making my net wide as the world
a muttering *lub-dub* of the heart, *lub-dub* of the sea,
starlings flash silver, hundreds turn, suddenly invisible.
I gather-in foxes, voles and fishes
to fall like feathers from a pillow shaken in the morning,
shelter the plain, overlooked, forgotten
in all those gaps, those murmurings,
all those I loved and who loved me
for who knows what will be saved
as through one physical life the soul makes migration,
slips through all measurements or stitches?

ONE FOR SORROW

Sleekly oriental
you swoop:
jack-hammer beak
enjoys its skill

having feasted
on grief
you leave orbs
unyolked on the path,

long pendulum of feather
a flash of blue black
you track me
all along the wall:

enamelled in your eye
I am your likeness,
my family all gone
but you are constant

I mount you on my thumb
spit to test the wind:
which way home,
executioner?

CLAST
From the Greek klastos, *to be broken*

I would be one of the stone-carriers at Ise,
one of the three hundred thousand who lift
white river stone hand by hand
from the old shrine to its new ground.

There are hands you know so well they are practically
 your own.
I am thinking of you today, thinking about your hands.
How long it is since I have held them.

Why did we leave the road north, for the sea and Catterline?
I found two stone halves there, turned them over
glistening red as pomegranate.
What cut them?
I've taken the ones I chose to keep with me ever since.
I keep them because they never change.

The feldspar of that coast, its rose
porphyry, conglomerate of ancients.
What is there to write? To be written,
torn up, rewritten,
paper / scissors / stone?

Ise half-reveals, half- conceals the presence of those
whose mystery is their residing in ordinary things.

Your hands, how they age around warts that remain
 unchanged,
immune to chemicals and remedies, nubs of surprisingly
 hard flesh
in eldritch humps and circles, something not in our
 language.
You asked: *why is this red in my heart?*

Laurencekirk, Dunnottar, Montrose, Johnshaven: do
 names possess spirits?
St Mary of the Storms, leaning, salt-worn. St Ninian,
stepping out of his boat.

Are stones not beautiful? I would go back to examine
 them again, to turn more over, release each into its
 light, its moment.

DARK STARLING

He is a bird taken from his nest
my mother says,
dark starling lone among peelly-wally gulls.
Often he is blue from cold and beating.

Strange, yet not kenspeckle –
familiar as our path from door
to door, as the way home,
lit or in darkness.

He calls his home *Grenada*,
tells me memories
I can't forget in my fetching and carrying
when brine burns my cut skin
and that weary engine never stops groaning.

I think of what forms slow
almost invisible
from the misty scum
we tend with our lifetimes.

Smoke blackens our tongues
and blasts our garden, but what it makes
sparkles so pure
only fine hands can touch it.

Black Tom is owned but in body,
my father says. Under the kirk roof
they sprinkle his holy soul so he is David Spens
and we are his brothers and sisters now: giving

all we can spare, coins from apron-corners,
enough to let that starling fly,
blue-dark glitter of a wing
in sudden glad light.

SOUTHERNNESS POINT

Fair warm here today
the man at the end of the narrow track agrees.

Winter shimmers behind him:
so much light pours into my eyes

all I can see is dark, the camera lens fills up with it
thick as rock-pool soup.

This is as far as it goes,
shore frayed as old underlay

with sea-thrift and willow-herb
and lastly, the lighthouse

stout in a faded waistcoat of creams, snuff browns,
buttons of sea-faded rust, great-uncle Stevenson –

finding here a thousand blues, mussel shells' old willow
smithereens, is to walk back and back

as if a man still watched from behind the light
and you yourself were a lonely message brought here by
    the sea.

STUMP AND PHANTOM

hunger for each other,
like twins separated at birth
dream furious dreams.

No happy endings
or ever after,
no discovering that across the border

everyone speaks their language.
Just a painstaking journey to a room
where inch by inch Recovery unsheets the mirror.

SMEUSE

Deep inside, the wind can't reach me
here. Moment in the day's passage

of more than rest – blessing of being unseen,
muscle and spring no more. In the high spires, others lift

along the line but I was made for this earthed life,
curious through mansions of roofless rooms.

Solitary mostly, it comforts me to know
these ways through, worn to the shape of our backs

where our kind has gone before: I fill
them, these gaps, not as they were filled

before: I go
into the white hereafter, about our business.

NOBODY'S DAUGHTER

Pain stuns everything:
I'm eleven again, sinking gin
from my mother who says I'm cursed.
Body I don't know you,
engine racking first-time pains
red labour-cramps I thought I had forgotten.
I am nobody's daughter, hardly even human now,
saying goodbye beyond touch or consolation
the way our old dog lay down to her dying,
grey muzzle warm and heavy on my thigh.

LUPIN TEA
for JPM

You pull the pods
like clip-on earrings from a lobe,

stir them in the pot with leaf-spines
and snail grit from the bandaged garden tap

till they go grey, like squashed kisses:
left to mash, we mooch in giantess heels,

offer each other pink and lilac filter-tips
from a crayola packet, blow *moues* of smoke.

Indoors the phone rings unanswered,
something vanishes, we don't know

if our father's watching fitful from his study or
if our mother's sleeping it off

so we play harder, lift dolls' cups
to our mouths, gag on the brew

that tastes of graves, not bitter
but black-sweet, like sloes

we have not yet tasted, the kick
of spirit, the women we will become.

SISTER

I stole skeins of your hair
from our hairbrush
just as I took
stuff you left around
that smelled of you, owned your mystery.

You were who I could never be.
I was the one who cried
in the only wordless hour
we sat as a family
before the shrink:

years you talked for me,
coping, coping.

I'm sorry for all of it,
the unmothering, unfathering,
the hurt that felt like love
and how I love you now

as we grow old on the far sides of separation.

IN THE FOURTH MONTH

you-dot in yolk
dark snag in the flare nebula
my body the light bulb
that burned you up
my want the dark matter crowding
your feeble constellation
so one by one each cell fizzles out,
we crash in bloody sea-swell.
I surface without you.

ZOETROPE

All night the cisterns whisper.
A lantern on its long chain
ticks and mutters in the stairwell,

something in the roof-light
breathes and blanches
where the story hung.

There are scuff-marks over the floor.
The child I was crosses the landing,
a torch swings round, sudden

galloping alphabet of silverish
fingerprints – all night I pick at the roof catch
as if I could spring it open.

HANDSPEAK

for the poet Luljeta Lleshanaku

The deaf woman makes houses with her hands.
Meaning is real, she says, *look, it hangs in the air*
and holds its shape.
Each word depends for its life
upon its brother and sister.

Today I thought of you
in the same breath.
For you, too, words are hard-won.
They taste of metal-plated rain, of loneliness, of smoke.
Stubborn, they refuse to yield.

Monumental, womanly,
They embed themselves in my body.

BLOTTO

On Starbucks' corner hunched against the cold
I've been here since the moon was high;
come morning, blow hard into the knot
of my blue hands, I have no hope
today will be more than the old shuttle
between being sober and being blotto.

It's a kind of leaving without going, blotto:
an easy travelling farther away than cold,
swift and sure as a loom shuttle
I go clean and I go high,
way past being lost or found – in hope
only that one day I shall free this knot,

memory-knot, hunger knot, knot
that's the opposite of blotto –
if you see me huddled at your feet I hope
you'd throw me more than a blind cold
stare from your important walking, high
above me, on your commuter shuttle:

to and fro you go, slaves of that great shuttle
faster and faster and for what? A slimy knot
you can never shift from your gut. Only a high
ending and a hurrah and I'll soon be blotto,
my fanfare in your face, my joke against life's cold
shoulder, in the sure and resounding hope

of what must come, hope in spite of hope.
The north wind's a blade-sharp shuttle
I'm an impediment to its purpose, cold.
All in the end I've got is this ordinary knot
That's me. Do you know blotto?
Do you know high?

Out cold, high, face kicked to a knot,
small hope of recovery. Found by the airport shuttle, blotto.

NIGHT DRIVE

Dark flies at our back. Light is draining into western hills, violet and brown smudges that soak to black while we look away. Small houses rear up on bends in the road, windows lit then lost, snapshots of home seen before the page is turned in a stranger's album.
We make a rushing tunnel of grey between hedgerows, we follow ourselves through like winged things in a spider's web. The eyes of cattle, staring open at the night, glitter and flare. We might be deep under the sea or flying out past the curve of the earth towards Antarctica. For the badger slipping from a ditch we are a momentary leap of the heart then gone.
I think of cows standing through the night, staring into what they cannot see.
The sudden flash of their gaze in ours. Their stillness and our hurry. How we look and look out through our small lives to the dark.

Seen from the night road
a shirtless man holds a child
in the lit kitchen

HAIR SHIRT

He sits hunched in the middle of the kitchen
on a hard chair. Too frail to get to the barber
he isn't sure I can do it. The thing in my hand, heavy,
wobbles when I follow his instructions, keep the teeth
close to the curve of his skull, push against the grain
as strands rise, lift like smoke, thistledown,
settle as grey / albino snow.
I have to imagine myself making *a good job*
all the while skimming his thin pink bone,
the old yellow roses of his ear without a nick,
a slip. One millimetre away from disgrace, always.
But now transformed, power – handed,
I'm erasing his pride to bare a newborn's head:
no blood is spilled, not much said, around us
in the end only a circle of feathers,
the remains of a spell.

Later I wonder why I ache and itch, each
movement I make a nettling, luxuriant, like shame.

HEN PARTY, MEXICO CITY

I'm given paper cocks and pink chorizo
to hang on a line over a small girl dozing,
school shoes dangling from her toes.

Someone turns the music up,
flips on all the lights. Every window
instantly goes black. We play pin-the-prick

on a cardboard hunk, dizzy with being twirled
in a satin blindfold. He ends up studded,
fantastical. I think of the yard dogs outside,

their noisy longing. Everything is sugar, brittle,
I am drinking too much strong liquor.
Mute stranger in the middle

I wonder how these women desire
and are desired, in their quiet,
in their secret bodies.

Someone screams: everyone leaps back.
I can't follow the yelling then I'm shown
a mother scorpion and the wet black

tangle of her babies discovered in a corner,
too slow to escape the furies who smash
each tiny head in turn with their kicked-off shoes,

heels turning grey with spatter, then wildly
shoot hissing arcs of fly-spray so we choke
and weep till all that's left, borne away to the dogs
on the flat of a shovel, is a dark mush of nothing.

SAD JAGUAR

The sad jaguar stalks Insurgentes Sur,

    her sleeping body left in the menagerie
    hardly knows she's gone but for a breath
    of warm night sticky with mango skins
    to tremble her eyelashes and whisper of lightning,

    is in no hurry to meet Santa Muerte
    who glitters eyeless in her tree-bole shrine
    or the street-sleeping guardian's dark
    presence if she comes too close –
    so swerves towards The Angels Club,

    steps through a circle offering of maize, chains
    and chicken blood at the hash-sweet entrance
    while girls get shipped on by the back door
    in low slung motors dark as liquorice,

    can be last seen by the Inquisition arch
    slipping between white-dipped trees whose roots
    lift and split the pavement stones into small volcanoes.
    She is making for the avenue of the dead,
    will arrive by morning.

WHAT REMAINED OF THE WEDDING CAKE

In midwinter's
thickening endometrium
I begin to dream again of the old house
its soft unsorted helpless things
wools, papers, words
still to be saved or forsaken

and the windowless
almost-room
of the 'drinks cupboard'
behind the stair in the deep
hurt of the house
where the chest freezer
purrs. Lit by one bulb
I enter again
this shelved cave
(swaddled and lagged
muffled with carpet-cuts
dust stippling glass)
a child has no word for,

kneel at the tarnished tin altar
that travelled to Africa and back
sealed eternally,
never to be moved or mentioned.
It emits its cold light,
planetary as neon.
I burn to touch it,
to raise the lid
of the tomb,
breathe in the blue spores
before air turns
to anti-matter.

BACK TO BALTIC STREET
for my Grandmother, Elisabeth Littlejohn Crowe Fenton

Her keys know me by my stranger's grip.
The lock resists at first, damp
has slowed its turn, but finally I'm in,
pause on the threshold, need to decompress,
see what I always remembered first,
the blue and yellow vessel on its slipway
faded from years of upturning, emptying,
counting. She lived all her life on this northern coast;
what the sea wanted, the sea took
yet against worst odds she believed in saving.

It's not her reading glasses, library books,
water unmoving in the pipes, beyond the hall
the colder and darker corridors
but what I know with my child's hands
as I push a penny in to make the boat go down.

CLOOTY GOSPEL

Winter labour – sacking washed, stretched and sewn
to frame's webbed edge, ready for the hook:
aad claes summer-gathered cut to stripes
kept spiral-rolled by colour, navy, worsted, black,
once-Sunday-bests of chintzes, slub, forget-me-not:
now we ink in snarled with supple elements, dot
after dot round saucer's curve, unfurl the track
that, snaking out from curl and twine of leaf, delights
how border, wave, cloud, flow together – look!
unsundered all and whole, the new Farne grown:

slow in furrow the riddled land begins to sprout,
shoots pushed in, hooked out, take chance and bloom
mosses, marram grass, seacoal under weathered hands,
pylon and turbine, windblown tethered mares,
tormentil, northerlies, otters and seals' slicked necks
mewl of cormorants and lambs, our wantings and regrets,
stave, blade, spiral, all of it a readying for prayer –
as a causeway also silvers then grows dull in tidal lands
so Eadfrith's swan-quill pricked out from the gloom
low saffron hillsides, lapis lazuli of high tides slipping out –

you would be happy, Cuthbert, sinking each
poor ulcerated foot deep into these springy tufts, your palms
soothed by cool, tweeded streams, your way
befriended, peopled, made fresh anew
by our labour around the frame, and in the weave
we offer fishing twine, star-grey Cuddy's beads,
(take our turn, our time, knowing we have so few,
only, all of us, our each allotted days),
kiss of indigo on calfskin, shells singing their inward psalm –
use these gifts, Cuthbert, gathered from your beach.

SUITCASE BABY

I was born on a black-hearted day
by a railway line and a silver lava road.
She laid me down in my grease / her blood
upon the pearlised lining, swaddled
in her camisole. My head touched the pouches'
chilly edges of her plated cigarette case
and Psalms. I breathed dust at each corner,
crumbs of grey hydrangea, tattered clues of hair.

I remember everything. The weave above my head
once blue as a starry chapel. The smell of leather
and antiseptic. Locks like castanets.
Of course I grew, tested the boundaries.
From rooming house to rooming house
she smuggled me in, set me out
under my battered canopy.
I can see for galaxies from here, right back
to the lone sperm
as it wheedled to be sucked inside
the four pillars of my deliverance.

'SCISSORS GIVE BIRTH TO SCISSORS'
A print by Louise Bourgeois, 1990

I am running a pair of blunt
dressmaker's blades across the chest
of a Crombie coat. I slit it
west, north, east, south
into slithers of snake-nest across the floor.
When I begin, there's no
salvage of buttons or searching pockets: I know
too many sad things, saturated, damp,
smelling of cooking oil, the fusty seats of buses,
that never worked out or came to nothing.
I strip slant and down. I am the black hole,
mother to unidentifiable remains.
Behind me a man who harms children stands in my
    shadow.
I smell burn and lime, layers of lining and wool
expose themselves, loll wide, so many floors and ceilings
in that bombed apartment block.
He says I will be sorry. I say
I have worn him for too long.

DEPARTURE

The silence that roars through threadbare stations!
In slants of light a woman sweeps yesterday's spores
from coat seams, paper money's greasy epidermis,
whispers of unfinished conversation,
across the silken platform –

and always coming closer, approaching
from the east, the border's
sleekness wants to grab you,
eat you, every cell, every flicker of your brain,
the language of your skin…

If all leave-takings could be put end to end, *positive /
negative /* a spine of narrow carriages
you could sway through, some hung with stalactites
some stuck dark with feathers, some a-clatter, business-like,
some mourning sibilants abandoned, ahistorical;

if we could make that journey!
I shape words inside my mouth short-lived as smoke
but even so, a kind of space. Walls, roof, floor,
plain wooden seats, a window, real against the drop,
the slide through grainy noise, running and running –

how to end with grace when you turn away, alone?
Your life pared down only to this moment,
a snowfall's white nothing, a sleep:
here is the point you disappear, the train
moves quietly along its length, a fog consumes itself,

fed by broken parts
kilometre after kilometre before the border,
and nobody's waiting for you –
at the other end no kin of wishbones
only the kiss of this poem.

LAMBING

The men, exhausted,
are in for breakfast
and a thaw.
Mam makes them scrub
the slime and blood off first.

They leave their truck
squint across the yard.
East wind burns,
I'm not allowed
but I peer over.

They are only
hills with eyes
like Holy Island
at first light

but there's a knot,
spat-out gristle
curled inside itself
and the almost-blue cord

that pulses from it to its mother
reminds me how
the causeway looked before

we'd taken a last chance and run
through sky we thought was water.

AGAINST HATE

Sole passenger on an early morning tram
I'm half asleep when the driver brakes,
dashes past me, dives into a copse of trees,
gone for so long I almost get out to walk.
Then he's back, his face alight,
I saw the wren! explaining
how he feeds her when he can
and her restless, secretive waiting.
We talk of things we love until the station.

I tell him of the Budapest to Moscow train
brought to a halt in the middle of nowhere,
everyone leaning out expecting calamity
but not the engine driver, an old man,
kneeling to gather armfuls of wild lilies,
orchids. He carried them back
as you would a newborn, top-heavy, gangly,
supporting the frail stems in his big, shovel hands.
These are small things, but I pass them on

because today is bloody, inexplicable
and this is my act, to write,
to feel the light against my back.

WHIRLWIND
>*for Remedios Varo, after her final painting* 'Naturaleza Muerta Resuscitando', *Still Life Reviving, 1963, Mexico City*

The table threshes its skirts
to deep crevasses
twisting, untwisting
in the throes of a death-dance tarantella

the inanimate meal
sanctified by love
offered to indifferent lips
levitates in fury:
tin plates career off,
rims flash, whetted knives
and flesh orbits
the vulva-like flame,
still point which may
or may not hold:

Mother of the séance you are
absent here only in
formalities.

We set our tables over and over
for the living and the dead
with living and long-dead
provisions, for Life,

that whirlwind at our back,
that wasps' nest, keeps
reviving us

for the next world and the next.

NOTES

p. 20 'Riddle with Two Answers':
1. A long marriage 2. A hedgerow.

p. 27 'I Think of You and Think of Skin':
This sonnet is in the voice of Anne Hathaway and refers to her father-in-law John Shakespeare who was a 'whyttawer', a worker in fine animal skin gloves.

p. 30 'Moleskins':
The Hungarian Jewish poet Miklos Radnoti was shot on a forced march in 1944. A notebook of poems was found in his greatcoat pocket when his body was later exhumed from a mass grave.

p. 42 'Mami Wata':
A West African goddess presiding over fresh and sea waters. She is also honoured in the African diaspora, in North and South America and the Caribbean.

p. 44 'Flower of Maryam':
The Resurrection Rose is used in the Middle East and North Africa as an aid to childbirth. The midwife places its dried twigs in warm water and it reconstitutes, opening and softening. Seeing this and drinking this water is said to dilate and soften the cervix.

p. 49 'Dark Starling':
Dark Starling, David Spens or 'Black Tom' was brought from the West Indies to Scotland as a slave by a Dr. Dalrymple. He was baptised in 1769 and eventually won his freedom due to wide support and fundraising from Fife churches, miners, salters and Edinburgh lawyers.

p. 52 'Smeuse':
   Dialect word for 'the gap in the base of a hedge made by the regular passage of a small animal'.

p. 67 'Clooty Gospel':
   The Lindisfarne Gospels are evoked in the context of a traditional Northumbrian craft, the making of 'proggy' or 'clooty' mats from old rags and clothes.

BIOGRAPHICAL NOTE

PIPPA LITTLE is a Scot born in Tanzania who lives in Northumberland. Publications include *The Spar Box* (Vane Women), a PBS Choice, *Foray* (Biscuit Press), *The Snow Globe* (Red Squirrel), *Our Lady of Iguanas* (Black Light Engine Room) and *Overwintering* (Carcanet Oxford Poets), shortlisted for The Seamus Heaney Centre Prize.

Her work has appeared in UK, American and Australian magazines (*TLS, Poetry Review, Magma, Ambit, MsLexia*) in many anthologies and online, on radio and on film. Collaborative work includes *Poetics of the Archive*, *ColmCille's Spiral* (Antiphonal), *Conversations Across Borders* and *The Written Image* (Scottish Poetry Library / Northern Printmakers). She has read at StAnza, Edinburgh, Wigtown and Durham festivals and in poetry venues in the UK, Eire and Mexico City.

She reviews poetry and has co-edited two Virago anthologies. She gives workshops and takes writing weekends. A member of PEN, she has been an Open University tutor and literacy development worker and, at the time of publication, is a Royal Literary Fund Fellow at Newcastle University.

Titles in Arc Publications'
POETRY FROM THE UK / IRELAND include:

D. M. BLACK
Claiming Kindred
The Arrow Maker

JAMES BYRNE
Blood / Sugar
White Coins

TONY CURTIS
What Darkness Covers
The Well in the Rain
folk
Approximately in the Key of C

JULIA DARLING
Indelible, Miraculous
COLLECTED POEMS

LINDA FRANCE
You are Her
Reading the Flowers

KATHERINE GALLAGHER
Circus-Apprentice
Carnival Edge
Acres of Light

RICHARD GWYN
Sad Giraffe Café

GLYN HUGHES
A Year in the Bull-Box

MICHAEL HASLAM
The Music Laid Her Songs in Language
A Sinner Saved by Grace
A Cure for Woodness

MICHAEL HULSE
The Secret History
Half-Life

CHRISTOPHER JAMES
Farewell to the Earth

BRIAN JOHNSTONE
The Book of Belongings
Dry Stone Work

JOEL LANE
Trouble in the Heartland
The Autumn Myth

SOPHIE MAYER
(O)

PETE MORGAN
August Light

MICHAEL O'NEILL
Wheel
Gangs of Shadow

MARY O'DONNELL
The Ark Builders
Those April Fevers

IAN POPLE
An Occasional Lean-to
Saving Spaces

JOS SMITH
Subterranea

PAUL STUBBS
The Icon Maker
The End of the Trial of Man

GEROGE SZIRTES & CAROL WATTS
Fifty-six

LORNA THORPE
A Ghost in My House
Sweet Torture of Breathing

ROISIN TIERNEY
The Spanish-Italian Border

MICHELENE WANDOR
Musica Transalpina
Music of the Prophets
Natural Chemistry

JACKIE WILLS
Fever Tree
Commandments
Woman's Head as Jug